Reframing
ADOPTION

A Christian-Based Birthmother
Grief Recovery Handbook

BY SHARON FOX

ABOUT THE TITLE

*M*y friend was a prolific painter in her later years. Her practice was to give each of her children pieces of her work at Christmas. One year she gave identical gifts that were 4" X 4" landscapes. She framed them in narrow dark frames. One of her children put the landscape on the bookshelf. Another put the painting on the dresser in the guest room. The third child reframed the landscape using a wide smooth frame and a large color mat. She hung it on the wall of her living room. Same picture as before—but now it was no longer in the shadows of a bookshelf or in a mostly unused space. It completed the decoration of an often used room.

Many of the attitudes held about Birthmother's roles have been in narrow "dark frames." They have been hidden on the back shelf of life or in inaccessible areas of life where they have been covered in the dust of secrets, shame, guilt, anger, and sadness. This book is dedicated to reframing the role of Birthmother. The choice of adoption for her child is no longer pushed to the back shelf of life experiences but becomes a part of the fabric of her life. To *gift* her child to another family through adoption is a brave action. All adoptions (open, semi open or closed) can be grieved in healthy ways. Open adoptions provide, in an appropriate way, the sharing of the joy of her child.

Closed or semi-closed adoptions have been the norm for many years. The grief of those Birthmothers may be magnified by the absence or diminished contact with their children and the adoptive parents. Sometimes, closed or semi-closed adoption is the right structure. No matter how the adoption was structured, the Birthmother will grieve.

Reframing Adoption©

May the future decisions of all Mothers be -
Gift or Guide,
<u>Gift</u> through adoption or
<u>Guide</u> the child as a parent.

Change the choice dialogue. Take abortion off the table. The choice for the child should be either *Gift or Guide*— by Gifting the child to another family or Guiding the child by parenting. This is a new choice that is realistic, healthy, and a blessed decision.

No more "Giving up", or "Surrendering", or "Relinquishing" a child. Think of adoption in a new way—to "**Gift**" a child through adoption.

The choice of Adoption makes a Birthmother Brave!

*T*his handbook is dedicated to Birthmothers. It is designed to provide support, understanding, and information to grieving Birthmothers, so that they may move from deep emotional loss to a renewed spirit of hope, joy, peace, and contentment. It is designed as a handbook to enable those who read it to actively respond to the information presented.

Brave Adoption Ministries, serving Birthmothers, Adoptive Families, Birth Families, and Adoptees and Bravely, a resource to Birthmothers, were founded by Heather Finney.

See our website WWW.BRAVEPENNY.COM for details on ordering more workbooks or programs and for donation opportunities.

The legalities

Adoption is a legal contract. Each state has carefully crafted its' law to ensure protection for all parties. Adoption participants may include all or some of the following: adoption agencies, legal counsel, American Indian Tribal Counsel, social workers, welfare workers, guardians, birthmothers, birthfathers, adoptive families, and a judge to complete a legal adoption. For open, closed, or semi-closed adoptions, the state has the welfare of the child as the primary focus. It is the responsibility of each participant to understand the adoption provisions set forth by the court.

ACKNOWLEDGMENTS AND CONTRIBUTORS

$\mathcal{W}$e gratefully acknowledge the contributions and assistance of the people who have shared personal information and resources with us in the development and preparation of this material. Names of the Birthmothers have been changed to honor their privacy.

Heather Finney, Birthmother and Inspiration for this handbook.

Paul Jones, Lay minister, Christ Church, Plano, TX

Thank you to Bill Pittenger, Dru Newman, Shirley Bowman, Marcie Roeschley, Diane Sanderson, the first read editors.

Deepest gratitude to Deborah Phillips who's editing skills and Spanish translation enabled this book to reach readers such as you.

Inspiration for the front cover design by Fran Roseberry.

Illustrations by Katie Arani

Thank you to Marilyn Muecke, Carolyn Pittenger, The Board of Brave Penny and the Weaver Sisters for praying me through this process.

To my husband, Jim Fox, who has blessed me with unwavering support and brought me joy beyond description.

INTRODUCTION

*T*his is a self-guided study of the unique grief experience of Birthmothers. It focuses on the grief of the Birthmother in the decision to choose adoption (either open, closed, or semi-closed) and gift her child to create another family. This is a Christian-based guide to understanding the grief process. For those Birthmothers who did not or could not choose open adoptions, the grief experience is felt in the same way. This is a handbook for all.

With great love there is sacrifice. When there is sacrifice, there is often Grief and Joy. How do you cope with the grief resulting from such a precious gift? The gift of your child to another family brings complex and profound emotions and issues. It is our prayer that this guide will help the reader understand the process of grief and aid in her coping with the complexities of the brave decision to enter into an adoption and find joy in the experience.

Heather Finney,
Birthmother, Founder of Brave Adoption Ministry

Sharon Fox,
Author, Lay Minister, Certified Grief Facilitator, American Academy of Bereavement

Open Letter

Dear Birth Moms,

*Y*ou do not have this book in your hands by some strange act of randomness—God put it in your hands so you can have some choices. After nine months and hard labor, you have brought forth a new life into this world. You now are holding the keys to abundant life for more than just yourself. Ladies, the whole process of life happens from your everyday small choices. The small choices you make each day have negative or positive results that are unseen in the moments they are made. These subtle choices compound over time.

I hope and pray you will choose the path that is less traveled, today as well as all the days to follow. The choice to heal from grief is easy to make: it's also easy *not* to make. The choice is yours and yours alone to make. In the years to come, grief can either become your lifelong pain or it can be transformed to contentment.

Sincerely,

Heather Finney

TABLE OF CONTENTS

PRAYER OF ABUNDANT LIFE

Oh God, how great You are!
Your love is unfailing,
Your mercy is new each day.
Never will I walk alone,
For You are always by my side.
When I am weak, carry me.
When the pain is deep, cry with me.
When I make the big mistakes,
Cover me with Your amazing grace.
As I walk the "road less traveled,"
Will You remind me moment by moment
You have walked it too?

Heather Finney

Brave Adoption Ministries, founded by Heather Finney, is committed to open adoptions whenever possible. Recognizing that open adoptions may not be applicable in every situation, the goal in any adoption is God's best and highest provision for the child and the Birthmother.

The enemy is attacking Birthmothers around the world to bring an end to adoption. He uses a Birthmother's grief as a way to speak lies into her heart. When Birthmothers believe these lies, their hearts become filled with shame and condemnation, which leave a wake of anger and doubt.

> **The gifting of a child is only possible if Birthmothers exist. Without Birthmothers, there could not be adoptions.**

Our focus is to speak Gods' truth to Birthmothers concerning their choice of adoption. We wish to enable God's Word to transform their hearts. Through the leadership of God and wise council, God's truth will be a light overshadowing darkness. Let God's light illuminate the path of healing.

Open adoption demands commitment, forgiveness, and communication from the Birthmother and the adoptive parents. Communication allows each child to know their biological history and enables understanding of the love in which they were gifted to the adoptive parents. It releases the common issues experienced by the child and the adoptive parents when an adoption is closed. We look to the biblical model of Moses, which was actually an adoption story, to help understand God's plan and provision through adoptions.

BIRTHMOTHER TO BIRTHMOTHER:

WHEN I READ THE SECOND PARAGRAPH ABOVE, I ACTUALLY TEARED UP! THE EVIL ONE TRIED AND STILL DOES WITH ME TO SPEAK LIES INTO MY HEART. I CHOOSE TO LISTEN TO TRUTH! JORDAN

A BIBLICAL MODEL OF OPEN ADOPTION

THE STORY OF MOSES

Exodus 2:1-10

The book of Exodus, in the Old Testament, tells the story of Moses. The story mirrors many of the elements common to the story of Birthmothers who choose open adoption. Moses became a great leader with a compassionate heart, but his birth and adoption story tell how simple acts of courage and obedience lead to God's fulfillment of His promise to bless and protect those who are brave.

Jochebed was a Hebrew woman and already a mother when this story begins. The political attitude about

Hebrew children was influenced by a ruler who was not a believer in Jehovah God, and feared loss of his political power with the population growth of the Hebrew people. The ruler took steps to influence the population increase and directed midwives to kill all male Hebrew babies at birth. Some of the midwives stood up to him and saved the babies even though the ruler disregarded the lives of these precious children. When the ruler realized he could not control the population using the midwives, he ordered his army to seize the male babies and throw them into the Nile River to die.

Jochebed gave birth to a son during these terrible times. She sought God's wisdom and put together a plan to save her baby. It was a plan that shows us how adoption is God's provision. In her plan, she placed her son in a basket that she put into the tall weeds by the edge of the Nile River. The basket was placed away from the swift water to float near the shore where it could still be seen. As a loving mother, Jochebed did not allow her baby to be swept away to certain death.

A woman of royalty, in fact the daughter of the ruler who was trying to kill the babies, saw the basket when she went to bathe in the river, and had it brought to her.

She saw the baby and immediately wanted him as her adopted son. She named him Moses, meaning "drawn from the water." Moses, as mentioned above, had other siblings. His sister, Miriam, was watching from the shore and asked the ruler's daughter if she would like someone to help with the care of the baby—she would need a woman to nurse the baby, because there was no other way to feed a baby.

Thus, a partnership of birthmother and adoptive mother was formed. Two women shared a child through an early form of Adoption. Miriam, although still a youth herself, was obedient to God's call to facilitate an open adoption by connecting the two mothers.

Moses was the gift, the ruler's daughter was the adoptive mother, and Jochebed was the caring Birthmother.

CHAPTER 1

DEFINITIONS OF GRIEF:

Although most adults and children have experienced grief, it can be difficult to understand when thinking about the choice of adoption of a child. Here is what grief is and is not:

GRIEF: NOT A PROBLEM TO BE SOLVED.

GRIEF: NOT A SITUATION TO BE OVERCOME.

GRIEF: IS A NATURAL RESPONSE TO THE LOSS OF SOMETHING WE LOVE.

In an open adoption, the Birthmother does feel the loss of her child. She has exchanged the dream of nurturing her child for one of sharing the child with another mother who will nurture the child instead. In the case of closed adoption, the loss is more acute. Recognizing that grief is a natural response and understanding it is the way God wired humans to experience these complex reactions to loss allows us to accept grief as a normal occurrence. Grief is complex, emotionally painful, and difficult to recover from for anyone who experiences it. We do not choose to grieve—we feel grief as an unavoidable experience when loss has occurred. Grieving should not be an embarrassment or source of shame—it is a normal emotion. God's nurturing words in Scripture show He understands our pain.

Do not let your hearts be troubled; believe in God, believe also in Me. - John 14:1 NAS

A woman giving birth to a child has pain because her time has come; but when her baby is born she forgets the anguish because of her Joy that a child is born unto the world.–John 16:21 NIV

> *Trust,* a simple word, a huge commitment. Birthmothers trust in God.

No safety net or guarantees about the future. "All in" equals trust in God's provision.

God's Model of Grief

What the grief process looks like and feels like:

God grieved the death of his son. In the Gospels He modeled for us how mankind would experience grief. All who grieve from a profound loss will experience the same pattern. At His Son's crucifixion, notice what happened:

- **Friday** — Darkness, an earthquake, and the fabric of life is torn apart
- **Saturday** — The Sabbath, a time of recovery
- **Sunday** — Resurrection to new life

These three days mirror elements that form the grief pattern. The grief model begins the day Jesus died. It was a Friday (in the afternoon). This may be the day that a Birthmother leaves the birth center without her child. However, grief events may have also occurred at other points of the journey. The onset of major events can be described as the "Friday" of the grief pattern. Keep in mind that God created the heavens and earth in six days. His grief model was accomplished in three days. It will take us much longer to process the loss felt when adoption is chosen, but the pattern is true when applied to any loss event in our lives.

Let's take a closer look at God's model:

Friday: Darkness as experienced in sadness and a feeling of loneliness

Friday—Darkness, an earthquake and the fabric of life torn apart.

When we review God's model of the grief process and the pattern when He mourned the death of his son, Jesus, we can see from Scripture that three significant things happened on the Friday afternoon of Christ's death. There was darkness, there was an earthquake, and the curtain in the temple was torn from the top to the bottom.

All three of those are descriptors of the initial stages of grief.

The first is darkness. It takes the form of sadness or the *dark cloud* that feels very overwhelming in the early hours/days/weeks/months after the decision to choose adoption has been made. Often feelings like profound sadness, and even depression, confusion, and fear are felt, and they are normal. The life-changing decision that has been made affects the Birthmother, the child, and the adoptive parents. Understand the darkness to be a part of the journey. Move through it. In Psalm 23 the reference to "the valley of the shadow" reflects the feelings a Birthmother experiences as she walks through this valley of life. (See Chapter 8 to read Psalm 23.)

The second is an earthquake. It takes the form of the *shaking* of all that we once expected in life. The things that were assumptions of trust, the bed rock of family values that have been cast for you or by you, now tremble and feel unstable. Often questioning the vision of the future, a Birthmother must realize that God had other plans. Trust Him to redefine the future from that day forward.

The third is the fabric (of life) is torn apart. In the Temple, which was a holy building used as the center of worship for the Jews, was a small area called the "Holy of Holies." It was considered a very sacred place where the church leaders, the High Priests, entered to pray. A curtain, four inches thick by sixty feet tall, hung at the entrance of this sacred place of worship. When Jesus died, the curtain was torn completely apart from top to bottom.

The only thing equal in life is our 24-hour day. Everyone has the same 24 hours. What we do with those hours has been granted in the form of free will to each of us. The tapestry of our life is the weaving in of events and people in the form of *threads* into our vertical hours and minutes. Some events and people are vivid, some are present for a season, and others are the stable threads that hold our lives together. Events occur in life that snip those threads. Occasionally, it feels like a huge hole has been cut in the fabric. Usually, a significant grief event feels like scissors have cut

> **For those who grieve, the torn curtain represents the fabric of their life being torn apart.**

away a piece of our life. The weaving that existed when they were in our life (such as the pregnancy period) feels like a huge loss when a baby is gifted instead of guided. There are certain steps that need to be taken when a hole has been cut into the fabric to prevent unraveling. One must bind the hole with threads. "Circling" in and around the hole will stabilize the integrity of the rest of the fabric.

It is important to understand that adoption can be like a hole in the life of a Birthmother that needs to have time spent processing or stabilizing the fabric, so that the rest of the tapestry of life can continue to be woven. It is also important to know that God calls us to bind the hole—spending time to regain balance and perspective of the decision. A Birthmother needs to start to gently weave new threads or continue incorporating threads of hope into the fabrics of life that will create the new portion of the tapestry yet to unfold. In a full view of life, the repaired hole becomes a part of who the Birthmother is—not the centerpiece from which she never really moves on. She is to live as God would have His children to live. A life with contentment and joy is a life that has mended holes.

Creating a new pattern of life that can be understood as normal, demands that there will be new threads woven into the fabric of life. There will be threads that end as well as the new ones that will be introduced. The look and feel of life takes on a new texture. With conception, gestation, and birth, the Birthmother introduces a child into the pattern of life. These new threads are usually woven into the remaining tapestry of the mother's life. Those threads have a different color and thickness for a Birthmother who has chosen adoption. They can end abruptly where a hole has formed as well. Adoption may also create unexpected thin spots or add in new thread patterns that impact the rest of the life of the Birthmother and the Birthmother's family.

SATURDAY: THE SABBATH

Sabbath—A time of recovery
God's Plan for Resting in Him and Healing Your
Wounded Soul

The observation of the Sabbath in the Jewish faith is still the same today as it was in Jesus' time. At sun down on Friday, the Sabbath begins. It lasts for 24 hours until sun down on Saturday. The observation of the Sabbath requires stopping all work, including meal preparation, and even driving a car. It is a time of worship and rest. When we look at the events of Friday afternoon at the crucifixion, the actions of the guards reflect the preparation for the Sabbath. They pierced Jesus' side to be sure he was dead, so that they could bury him before the Sabbath began. We, too, need to do the work that has to be done and then rest. Our society does not allow us much time off to grieve. Many places of work have a maternity allowance for time off. That time off may not be available or long enough when adoption has been chosen. It places the Birthmother in a situation requiring her to return to to work, school, or other responsibilities sooner than would be ideal. Physically recovering from birth and yet still struggling with the emotional stress of the adoption helps us to understand the reason that God modeled a Sabbath in the pattern of grief recovery.

It is essential that a Birthmother recognize that rest, recovery, and permission to be in a recovery mode are the quickest bridge to stability for her new life pattern. The Birthmother can ease out of the darkness, reestablish new foundations of life, and weave a new daily pattern of life. Careful planning and perhaps negotiations need to be considered with options explored for everyone's benefit when addressing maternity leave for a Birthmother.

> **Take time to grieve. Heal from the inside out. There is not a "skip-to-the-front-of-the-line" secret. Healing is an important step to perspective, judgment, and contentment. You can be a wonderful role model to your child, the adoptive parents, and others when you have taken the time to heal, which is the road to finding a life of contentment.**

BIRTHMOTHER TO BIRTHMOTHER:

THIS IS SO TRUE. HIDING GRIEF WILL ONLY HURT YOU MORE! JANE

SUNDAY: THE RESURRECTION

Resurrection—A Transformed New Life

The third element of God's model is finding the new being, the new chapter, and the new life, where the Birthmother not only survives, but thrives. It is important for the Birthmother to recognize that she is forever changed—not in a bad way—and she is now different than when she began her journey. Jesus was seen many times as a "new being" after his Sunday morning resurrection. The Birthmother can find comfort and assurance as she sees this is part of God's plan to make her a new being with a new heart and a soul that is healing.

A Birthmother's gift of her child to another family is beyond measure. The wisdom to gift a child is also beyond measure. No scale or yardstick or machine can measure the love and bravery of a Birthmother.

Create in me a clean heart, O God, and renew a right spirit within me.- Psalm 51:10 KJB

Christ rose from the dead. That act demonstrated to all

of us that even in the darkest, most difficult circumstances there is hope. That is God's promise, to walk
with every Birthmother and to hold her in His loving
arms. Jesus reached out into the lives of those who
knew him and assured them that He was who He said
He was ... God's son. If you are a believer in Jesus as
God's son who came to
earth to save us from our
sins and provide eternal
life, you are adopted too.
As a Birthmother, you
are an adopted child of
God. Jesus spoke of
brothers and sisters who
would join him in heaven
and share in the eternal

> **You will never forget,
> nor should you try to
> forget. It is your job to
> take responsibility for
> the rest of your life. To
> seek to live in content-
> ment and joy knowing
> that life is renewed and
> redeemed and blessed.**

joy. Adoption is everywhere! The adoption in this case
was provided by Jesus when he died to pay the price
for our sins.

When the disciples grieved, they did so as a commu-
nity of people who had a common loss. They gathered
together in the upper room and talked about their experience. Finding a support group, fellow Birthmothers,

or a trusted friend with whom you can share your Birthmother experience will help the healing in a healthy way.

Activity:

Where are you on the *three-day journey* through grief? Are you still on Friday? Have you eased into the Saturday Sabbath of rest, or have you found contentment and joy consistently in your life?

Journal in the space below where you feel you are in your *three-day journey* of grief recovery.

BIRTHMOTHER TO BIRTHMOTHER:

NEVER FEAR YOUR GRIEF! IT WILL HURT, BUT IT'S A HEALTHY HURT THAT WILL MAKE YOU SO MUCH STRONGER.

-JORDAN

I THINK REACHING OUT TO EACH OTHER IS VERY IMPORTANT. BUT UNDERSTANDING AS A PART OF SUPPORT IS ALSO IMPORTANT. ADOPTION IS A HARD TOPIC TO TALK ABOUT, IF OTHERS DON'T "GET IT." A LOT OF TIMES WHEN I WOULD MENTION IN THE PAST ABOUT MY ADOPTIONS, OTHERS WOULD RESPOND TO IT AS "HOW COULD YOU JUST GIVE YOUR BABY AWAY?" THEY DON'T UNDER-STAND THE PAIN THAT WENT BEHIND THAT

CHOICE. SO, KNOWING HOW TO RESPOND WHEN PEOPLE AREN'T SHOWING LOVE IN THEIR WORDS IS IMPORTANT TOO. YOU "GOTTA" BE CAREFUL ON WHO YOU LET IN. ESPECIALLY DURING THE EARLY MONTHS.

-ELIZABETH

CHAPTER 2

WHAT DOES GRIEF LOOK LIKE AND FEEL LIKE?

*G*rief has many complex aspects. The grieving Birthmother will find the following list of effects that are commonly experienced:

Profound sadness

Sense of emptiness

Anger

Guilt

Shame

Resentment

Un-forgiveness

Memory loss

Excessive Swallowing

There are many elements of grief. We have included a few key words or phrases with some background about how they affect the griever. This chapter's list of descriptors is to identify other feelings associated with grief. They are normal but unwelcome and not easy to accept. Know that you are not alone with these deep and burdensome feelings. Every person who has experienced a profound loss shares these types of common markers of grief. When a Birthmother recognizes that these types of feelings are normal, the feeling will become easier to understand. Understanding will give her a choice of how she deals with the feelings of grief.

PROFOUND SADNESS

Birthmothers usually experience sadness. Understand that this is normal and also understand that there are healthy ways to deal with sadness that will get you to

> **First you decide, then you act, then you live it out.**

a place in your life where contentment rather than sadness is the way you will live your life. Sadness can be your lifelong companion. Make the wise decision to choose a life of contentment.

Decide every day that today you will look for blessings throughout the day. Be thankful!

Act with respect for yourself and others. Extend a smile, a friendly gesture, and a compliment to at least one person every day. Take care of yourself! Do healthy things to keep your energy and attitude up.

Live in a pattern of thankfulness and positive actions every day.

The results will be less sadness and more contentment.

BIRTHMOTHER TO BIRTHMOTHER:

IN MY SADNESS, I WORSHIP! I LOOK BACK TO THE LORD'S PROMISES. I READ MY READING MY JOURNALS FROM WHERE I WAS TO WHERE I AM NOW.

-JORDAN

MOOD SWINGS WERE BIG TOO. ONE
MOMENT I WAS FINE, THE NEXT, CRYING
BECAUSE OF A SMELL OR SEEING A BABY. THESE
HAVE LESSENED AS TIME HAS MOVED ON.

-ELIZABETH

MY COUNSELOR TOLD ME SADNESS SHOWS
THAT I LOVE MY CHILD. GOD UNDER-
STANDS THIS SADNESS AND WANTS TO HEAL
IT. HE LOVES YOU. HE IS PROUD OF YOU. I
HAD COMFORT IN KNOWING THAT SINCE I
FOLLOWED GOD'S WILL, I GAVE MY CHILD
GOD'S BEST LIFE FOR HER. I NEVER WANTED
A GOOD LIFE TO REPLACE GOD'S BEST LIFE.

-MANDI

EMPTINESS

Birthmothers report that they feel like their "heart is empty". They feel the longing is much like "not completing a task" which they feel obligated to finish. Or that the heart is missing an element that is satisfying and pleasurable. The emptiness feeling is emotionally very strong and often leaves the Birthmother feeling incomplete.

GUILT AND ANGER

Guilt is a significant overwhelming feeling that can press into the life of one who grieves. Often, guilt and anger go hand in hand as twin feelings that can take over every action and thought of the griever. Guilt and anger are feelings that you can control. Remind yourself daily that you will not be captured by either guilt or anger, which would diminish your wholeness. If you feel guilt and anger, you are normal. It is what you do with those feelings that make the difference in your life. Reframe the guilt and anger. Think of those feelings as accepting the past and looking to the future with anticipation, hope, and contentment. God calls us to live full lives of contentment. He asks us to place our trust in His hand of provision.

You may ask, "What is there to be joyous about? I am a Birthmother and I have gifted my child to someone else." This is when the trust element comes in. Trust God to provide, protect, and bless your decision. As a Birthmother, you have no idea what plans the Lord has for your child.

> **I am a Birthmother. I chose life. I was obedient to choose to Gift my child. I am Brave! Trust God to provide, protect, and bless your decision.**

Trust God to do His grace-filled work in the life of your child, the adoptive family, and you. Rest in the peace that you were obedient in gifting your child and let God be the light for this journey.

Guilt can come from lots of different issues. For example, a Birthmother may feel guilty about how the pregnancy came about or for actions taken or not taken at conception. Guilt may also occur as she considers the effect of the pregnancy on her own family of origin.

BIRTHMOTHER TO BIRTHMOTHER:

GUILT AND ANGER HAVE BEEN VERY HEAVY FOR ME. MY GUILT IS ABOUT MY PART AND

ANGRY OVER NOT BEING ABLE TO CARE
FOR MY SON.

-JANE

SHAME

With Secrets Come Shame

Shame affects us like a dark cloak that is so heavy we cannot move forward into a life of grace and contentment. It is the unspoken judgment of society and a stifling self-imposed emotion for many Birthmothers. How can the cloak be pushed off of the

> It is OK to say: "How the conception occurred is very personal. The result of the conception was a blessing that I could share with another family."

shoulders and left behind? How can we reframe the brave choice of adoption as a solution that God blesses instead of a shame-based life choice?

Let us pray:

Lord, you know the heavy burden of shame that I carry. I am asking and now trusting you to lift that burden of shame. I desire to have a change in my heart and healing in my soul so that I can live a renewed life of contentment. Amen.

Only a few years ago, divorce was a source of shame for many people. Today, saying that divorce has occurred in someone's life is no longer shameful. Bring the discussion to be a Birthmother out into the open. Shine God's light on it.

> **Bring the choice to be a Birthmother out of the shadows of shame.**

BIRTHMOTHER TO BIRTHMOTHER:

SHAME IS FROM SATAN. THE LORD COUNTS NO SINS AND IS NOT LOOKING AT SHAME.

-JORDAN

RESENTMENT

There is a saying: "Resentment is the poison I drink in the hope that it will kill you." This is a startling statement when you recognize the implication. The worst part about the feeling of resentment is that it changes nothing! It simply poisons you! It is easy to fall into the trap of jealousy and resentment toward other women, the Birthfather (if he is not involved), the family that is raising your children, or the families that are untouched by adoption. It is easy to resent siblings or girlfriends who are free of the life-changing events that you as a Birthmother have experienced. Don't drink the poison. It harms you. Give up resentment!

BIRTHMOTHER TO BIRTHMOTHER—A PERSONAL PERSPECTIVE:

I WAS VERY RESENTFUL OF MY GIRLFRIENDS. THEY WERE LIVING A LIFE THAT WAS FREE OF JUDGMENT OF OTHERS. IN MY CASE, MY FAMILY WAS SUPPORTIVE BUT STILL HID THE FACT THAT I WAS PREGNANT AND HAD HAD A SON. ONE DAY I RECOGNIZED THAT

ALTHOUGH MY LIFE EXPERIENCE WAS CER-
TAINLY DIFFERENT THAN MY GIRLFRIENDS
AND MY FAMILY'S EXPECTATIONS, I KNEW
IN MY HEART THAT I HAD BEEN GIVEN A
UNIQUE GIFT. I HAVE HAD A LIFE EVENT OF
PREGNANCY AND BIRTH AND CHOICE OF
ADOPTION THAT HAS GIVEN ME WISDOM.
AND MOST IMPORTANT—A DEEPER RELA-
TIONSHIP WITH MY GOD.

-ANNA

FORGIVENESS

Forgive yourself and forgive others. You and everyone else in your life have done and will do things that need forgiveness. There are no exceptions. No one walks on the earth today who has not made mistakes or poor decisions!

Review the definition of Forgiveness on the next page. Fill in the blanks for whom and for what forgiveness is needed in your life. It is the best thing you can do for yourself today.

Activity:

I choose to forgive (names or initials) _____,

_____, _____, _____,

_____

I need to ask for forgiveness from (names or initials) _____, _____, _____,

_____

I choose to forgive myself for (unhealthy thoughts) _____, _____, _____,
_____

I need forgiveness from God for _____, _____, _____, _____,
_____

Now live in peace – You are forgiven.

Forgiveness is:

To give up my unrealistic expectations
To give up my right to be angry
To give up my right to blame
To give up my right to retaliate
To give up my attempts to control others
To give up my yearning for a better yesterday

Forgiveness is NOT:
Forgetting
Tolerating
Excusing

Minimizing

Rationalizing

Freedom from consequences

> **Choose to lift the heavy burden of Un-forgiveness from your life.**

THE MAIDEN AND HER ROCK COLLECTION

She was not sure how the collection of rocks began—perhaps from childhood or just because it felt so "right".... But the Maiden had a collection of rocks that she carried with her in a backpack for easy access. It was strapped over her shoulders and across her chest.

She added new ones from time to time. Often she took them out to display or exhibit, for others to see. Each time she handled them, they seemed to grow heavier and larger in size. Others saw them as ugly and responded by backing away immediately when she brought them out. She saw them as objects that identified her in a unique way. The rock collection was called "un-forgiveness."

Soon the backpack was expanded to the limit, so the Maiden unpacked the rocks and placed them on a platform. (Some called it an altar) so that she could have quick access to them when needed. The problem was that the rocks were so heavy and pushing them along the pathway of life was getting harder to do each day. Other folks on her pathway, she noticed, were moving along much faster and without a rock collection at all. She wondered about that. Her head was always down and she was always struggling to push and shove the collection along.

One day she paused to look about and saw some very interesting things. She had been so busy moving her rocks that she had failed to notice the lovely surroundings along her pathway. Flowers, trees, soft breezes, gentle waters, mountains, and ocean vistas ... all these wonderful things had been blocked from view by the high pile of rocks.

She was quite surprised to catch a glimpse of a building that sat beside the pathway she traveled. Funny she had been expending much energy on the rocks that she had just not taken note of the large sign mounted on top of the building that read "**Exchange Center.**" The building had been hard to see because of the tall mound of dirt that ran along the side of the road. She left the pile of rocks and scrambled over the mound of dirt to get a better look. The owner was standing at the door.

There was a sign in the window in bold lettering that read:

Exchange your Sins for Salvation.

Exchange Disobedience for the Blessings of Servant hood.

Exchange your Sorrows for Joy.

There was one that really got her attention.

Exchange your Burdens for Contentment and Rest.

It reminded her of the verse in Matthew. *"Come to me, all who labor, are weary, and heavy laden, and I will give you rest."* **NAS**

"Wow", the Maiden thought, this was just what she needed. She was exhausted from pushing the rocks along her pathway every day. If she understood the sign, she could trade in her rocks and receive a gift of rest and peace. That sounded really good to her!

"What are your hours, sir? I have some things to trade in," She said.

"I am always here – 24/7," He said.

"Have you never been away, ever?" She blinked.

"Yes," he replied "A long time ago, I was away from Friday afternoon until Sunday morning. Once I got back here though, I never left this doorway again."

"Oh!" she stared in amazement.

"As I said, I am interested in the Exchange Program you are offering. Could you just take *all* of my rocks over there in my pathway and give me one big gift of Contentment and Rest?"

"No," he replied. "It does not work that way." He paused. "You will have to bring each one of the rocks to me and tell me how you collected it and ask me to trade it in on exchange. One rock at a time, one gift of contentment and rest at a time." She was puzzled about that. She hurried over and picked up one of the small rocks and did the exchange right then and there. She told Him about the lady who was rude to her and she just could not forgive her at the time. But now, a long time later, it was time to forgive. The owner gave her the gift of contentment and rest. It felt like a comforting blanket around her shoulders. She felt better immediately.

Each day she brought more and more of the rocks to the **Exchange Center.** After confessing the story of the "un-forgiven rocks," she would receive another gift. Time passed and she was soon down to the Really Large Rocks. She was not so eager to exchange them for several reasons. She had had them for so long and they were big and very heavy. It seemed too hard to carry them over the roadside mound to the door. She was reluctant to trade them in. The mound, which she had nicknamed "Pride," seemed particularly high each time she started to take one of the really big rocks to the store owner. She would start off determined but would turn back because it was too hard. Several times she thought that she would just keep them, but she knew in her heart that she needed to trade them in.

Finally, with reluctance and with great effort, she moved the largest rock off of the altar and over the "pride" mound to the **Exchange Center.** The man stood at the door, as he always faithfully did, and welcomed her as she shoved the largest rock over to him.

"Why have you kept this rock for such a long time? Did you not realize how much better life would be if you had just brought it sooner?" he asked.

"I know that now, but "pride" kept me from it. And besides, I thought you didn't know about it," she said.

"Oh, I have known about it for a long, long time. I saw you pick up the rock the day you decided not to forgive. I saw it when you first put it into your backpack. I saw it when you made it the centerpiece of your altar."

She bowed her head and said, "I am sorry, sir."

He replied, "My name is Jesus and you are forgiven."

By Sharon Fox ©

Activity:

Meditate on the Rocks that are in your backpack. Is "pride" the obstacle that keeps you from forgiving others? Is un-forgiveness blocking you from peace? Follow the Maiden's example: Confess and let go of the rocks. Allow God to bless and heal your soul.

BIRTHMOTHER TO BIRTHMOTHER:

I THINK IT IS IMPORTANT THAT FORGIVE-NESS IS A CHOICE AND SOMETIMES YOU HAVE TO CHOOSE IT OVER AND OVER AGAIN. IT IS NOT ALWAYS EASY. IT WILL BRING REST AND CONTENTMENT.

-ELIZABETH

Memory loss

While your body is busy recovering from the birth experience and the important decision of adoption, your mind is also busy trying to carry on in a normal way. There seems to be a depletion of focus, often described as memory loss. A sense of memory loss is NORMAL after a profound life event.

> **A sense of memory loss is NORMAL after a profound life event.**

Do not be concerned if you struggle with an inability to think clearly or remember details. It does remind us that additional time to think through decisions and actions is needed to avoid disappointment later.

Excessive Swallowing

An interesting physical sign of stress is frequent swallowing. When attending a funeral excessive swallowing can often be observed in those who are experiencing acute grief. Excessive swallowing is also observed in those who are under extreme stress in non-grief related situations. Research has pointed to excessive swallowing caused by stress as a possible cause of obesity and substance or alcohol abuse. Swallowing is instinctual. Swallowing is a soothing human activity. As Adults, we need to be aware that the self-soothing act of eating and drinking, to excess, can occur. Comfort food does not solve the problem of emotional pain. Alcohol or other chemicals are poorly fitting bandages for the

> **It is important to recognize that food or drink to excess may serve a need to fill the emptiness or to quiet the emotional pain with destructive results.**

wounded soul. It is important to recognize that eating and drinking to excess may satisfy a need to fill the emptiness felt when there is emotional pain. Seek professional help if you are struggling with food or substance abuse issues. Alcoholics Anonymous (AA) or Over Eaters Anonymous (OA) have excellent support programs.

The impact of grief is based on two elements.
1. Suddenness
2. Intimacy

The length and depth of grief will be measured by both suddenness and intimacy. Nothing is more intimate than the connection of a mother to her child. Suddenness is the very short time typically between birth and the adoptive parent or agency's action of leaving with the baby. Therefore, the impact of the adoption process on the Birthmother will be profound and lifelong. It does not mean, however, that the Birthmother will have a life-long sense of sadness.

> **God did not promise life would be easy. He did promise to be with us. Leaning into God's promise that He will be with us is the goal of everyone who grieves.**

CHAPTER 3

ORIGINS OF GRIEF
FOR A BIRTHMOTHER

*G*rief for a Birthmother is defined as the sense of loss resulting from the choice to share the natural nurturing of her own biological child with another mother and family. There are also grief events that may occur much earlier than the actual day that the child is entrusted to the adoptive family or agency. Grief may come from one or more of the elements listed below:

1. Realization of possible pregnancy
2. Confirmation of pregnancy
3. Conversation with Birthfather
4. Conversation with family and friends
5. First doctor visit

6. Awareness of an estimated delivery date
7. Detection of movement of the baby
8. Hearing the baby's heartbeat
9. Identifying the sex of the baby
10. Recognition that adoption is an option
11. Initial discussion regarding adoption

This list indicates that there is not just one but several grief origin points in the choice to Gift a child. One grief origin may be reasonably fast to recover from while others may be very painful and last longer. Recognize that grief events are often clustered in life. It is important to examine each event and carefully review how they affect our lives.

Activity:

You may want to add other elements or events or realizations that have created a sense of grief for you.

1.

2.

3.

> **The brave step for a Birthmother is in sharing a child willingly and joyfully through adoption with another family. The courage is then finding a healthy way to be compassionate and honest in the adoption relationship.**

BIRTHMOTHER TO BIRTHMOTHER:

I FOUND THAT SHARING MY STORY NOW ABOUT OBEDIENCE AND WALKING WITH THE LORD, HAS HELPED ME HEAL A LITTLE MORE.

-JANE

HOW DOES GRIEF AFFECT A BIRTHMOTHER?

All areas of life are affected.
1. Intellectual balance
2. Emotional balance
3. Physical balance
4. Spiritual balance
5. Social/Relationships balance

Rebalancing life

Prior to the Birthmother's journey of conception, gestation, and birth, the elements of intellectual, emotional, physical, spiritual, and social relationships are usually in balance. We think, feel, physically function, live on a spiritual level, and have social relationships that make sense to us. No matter what type or the origin of loss, those elements become out of balance. Part of this guide is to help understand the need to rebalance and to learn to cope with the new normal of open (or closed) adoption. All of the intellectual, emotional, physical, spiritual, and social relationships are interrelated. As we examine the unique issues of the

Birthmother, there are other complex dilemmas that come into consideration.

INTELLECTUAL BALANCE

Why does a decision to gift your child (in the act of sharing through adoption) feel like the right one and yet the decision is such a difficult one at the same time?

Addressing this question will help to clarify the intellectual imbalance. Thinking and writing out responses will help to clarify these questions.

Activity:

Writing and thinking about two key questions will help you come to a peace with the intellectual decision.

1. Describe how *you* feel about the decision of Adoption.

2. Explain how you respond to others who question or want to know how you, as the Birthmother, came to that decision.

> **When asked about the role of Birthmother, reframe the response.**
>
> **"I was given a wonderful experience of carrying a baby during its first nine months of existence. I Gifted it into the lives of another family who desired a child to complete their family."**

EMOTIONAL BALANCE

Emotions are strongly connected to the hormonal changes in the female body as a part of the gestation/pregnancy process. These emotional elements are heightened to unexpected levels. Immediately after delivery, the flush of hormones in the Birthmother's body creates strong and sometimes erratic emotional feelings and responses to situations. Natural patterns of emotional highs, lows, and duration are impacted by the realization that a tiny life has been growing in the Birthmother's womb. These hormonal changes may cause the Birthmother to question the decision of adoption. Contentment and peace can feel out of reach to the Birthmother. Clear thinking maybe difficult at this time.

Activity:

Journaling is simply writing. Writing is a key element in the ability to process and move toward healing. It is not supposed to be a publishable piece of work. Actually, no one should read this journal except the author. Journaling is a unique method of putting down the feelings that seem to be the white noise of life. The volume of the tapes that will not shut off in our thoughts is toned down.

Journal your response to the following questions: (See the list on the next page of emotions that may be useful in this activity.)

1. List the new or stronger emotions that you currently have or recently experienced during the pregnancy.

2. List the new or stronger emotions you experienced at the time of the decision to gift your child through adoption.

3. List the new or stronger emotions you experienced at the time the transfer of your child to the adoptive parents occurred.

List of feelings experienced by those who grieve.

Self-pity	Small	Alarmed
Cheated	Solemn	Anxious
Sullen	Sorrowful	Apprehensive
Aggravated	Ugly	Awkward
Agitated	Unhappy	Dreadful
Bitter	Fortunate	Frightened
Burned up	Good	Guilty
Disgusted	Grateful	Horrified
Frustrated	Joyful	Intimidated
Furious	Lucky	Insecure
Grief	Okay	Nervous
Hopeless	Pleased	Overwhelmed
Hurt	Positive	Panicky
Inadequate	Relieved	Pressured
Lonely	Safe	Self-conscious
Melancholic	Satisfied	Shy
Miserable	Secure	Timid
Mournful	Thankful	Troubled
Pained	Thrilled	Worried
Regretful	Terrified	Uneasy
Rejected	Angry	Uncertain

Alienated

Baffled

Bewildered

Conflicted

In Denial

Disconcerted

Disconnected

Displaced

Entrapped

Embarrassed

Foggy

Flustered

Indecisive

Lost

Perplexed

Torn

Hostile

Irate

Mean

Negative

Outraged

Peeved

Raging

Resentful

Uptight

Abandoned

Blue

Bored

Dejected

Despondent

Depressed

Sad

Distressed

Dreadful

Loss of control is often described as the one key element that is missing in order to experience recovery from a grief experience. Write, speak, and think the words that reflect the way you feel. Naming or identifying the feelings experienced during the grief journey gives a sense of control. Use words to give you control of your feelings and your life again.

SHADOW GRIEF

Shadow Grief is a recognized form of grief response that is described as a sudden and strong emotion that feels overwhelming to the griever. A smell, a sound, a glance, even a memory flash that is shocking in its impact and emotional reaction creates a shadow grief event. A sudden change can trigger a strong emotional response of tears, sense of sadness, acute anxiety, or fear, which are often described by those that experience a shadow grief event. Shadow grief is normal. Although it may feel scary, don't be afraid or scared. When there has been a profound change or loss, there will be shadow grief events. They will be less impactful, less intense, and further apart as time goes on, but they will occur. Understanding how to respond when they do occur will give you a sense of control. Here is how.

Recognize that when you have a very strong emotional reaction to something, it is likely a shadow grief event. Usually, these events only last a few moments in duration. If someone is close by and sees you suddenly crying for no apparent reason, it is okay to say to them say: "I am having a shadow grief moment. Give me a minute. I will be fine." They will understand that you are regaining your composure and they will respect your honest statement.

Occasionally, shadow grief will take a different form just prior to a significant date. Instead of being momentary, a strong feeling that seems to be unshakable may last several days or even weeks. This is called anxiety-driven shadow grief. It is a sense of dread that a date is coming and the date will bring difficult memories or a stronger sense of grief. Generally, these are rare events. It is a comfort to understand that the next day after the date, the sense of loss will usually dissipate. Be patient. The pattern is for these events to lessen in impact. If very strong feelings linger more than a few days or do not decrease significantly or end after the date has passed, you may need to seek professional help or meet with your adoption counselor to discuss the emotions that are impacting your ability to function.

Will there always be life marker shadow grief events surrounding events such as the first tooth, first step, first word, first day of school, graduation, marriage, and so forth? These are life events. And no matter what the relationship of the Birthmother is to her child, these would be emotional events. Plan for them, look forward to them, celebrate them, and find joy in them. They are a part of being a mother, a Birthmother or an adoptive mother.

PHYSICAL BALANCE

During the pregnancy, the body undergoes many changes. Delivery, either natural or by C-section, is a body assault. Compound that with pain blockers, other medication, bones and muscles shifting, internal organs stretching and constricting, and hormones released—all create a chaotic physical condition. The recovery time to restore and regain normalcy is critical to the ability to cope in a healthy way with the new reality that faces the Birthmother.

> **When you take care to follow the medical recommendations, which will include balanced nutrition, resuming daily routines, resting, hydrating, and appropriate exercise, you will enable your body and your mind to cope with the changes in your life.**

EMPTY ARMS SENSATION

Empty arms sensation is a real and normal response. Not holding your child or the lack of contact physically may cause an aching sensation in your arms. You may long for a gentle pressure against your chest and have a desire for touch on your neck or face. Often described as an ache that has no origin, the recommended comfort is to cuddle something soft like a stuffed animal that will help to fulfill this need for physical contact. The action of holding, carrying and, even rocking a soft bundle

> **Recognize that an adoption is counter to how the natural body works after a delivery. There will need to be adjustments.**

during the first few weeks after delivery will help to calm the anxious and painful longing that are "empty arms" for a Birthmother. Some Birthmothers add a pet to their life. A cat or dog that seeks and enjoys physical contact could be a good option. These are not child substitutes, but they can be a comfort for the soul of the Birthmother.

SPIRITUAL BALANCE

Let's review God's model of grieving:

Friday afternoon, darkness, earthquake, fabric of our life torn apart

Saturday, the Sabbath, the resting time for the recovery of the body and soul

Sunday, the Resurrection, moving into the season of new context of living and contentment

Jesus was "different" after His resurrection. He was sometimes not recognized by His followers during the 40 days after that wondrous Sunday morning. He looked different and He was different. As a Birthmother, the new being is a complex combination of post-delivery, soul recovery, new relationships, and adjustment to a lifetime event into which

You are forever changed. You have chosen, for reasons that may or may not be expressible to others, to gift your child to another family. You are BRAVE. You are God's child. God will be glorified from this decision and gift.

you play the new role of Birthmother. Gifting your child to

a family who will nurture, guide, discipline, witness milestones, and assume parenthood is a generous blessing.

Grieve the loss of the role of mother as you transition to the new role of Birthmother during the Sabbath.

> **Jesus took the time to Grieve, and so SHOULD every Birthmother.**

WHEN JESUS GRIEVED

John, the Baptist was Jesus' cousin and a huge part of his ministry. He died violently. Jesus had been preaching all day to a group of followers when he got the news of the death. Jesus got into a boat and rowed into the Sea of Galilee where He spent time in the boat. Although we don't know exactly what He did as a part of his grieving, He probably thought about how this event was going to change his life, ministry, and family. He probably talked to His Heavenly Father in prayer and cried. He grieved over the loss. When he was ready, He rowed back to the shore and found the people were waiting for Him. Jesus had to decide to put the oars in the water and pull hard to come back to shore, that is what you, as a Birthmother, will need to do. Take time to grieve; think about how this will affect the rest of your life, and then make a decision to return to shore. Come back into the life and work that is waiting for you. Rejoin the fellowship of others. You can become comfortable with the new role of Birthmother. It will be hard work. But you can do it.

When Jesus heard what had happened, he withdrew by boat privately to a solitary place. Hearing of this, the crowds followed him on foot from the towns. When Jesus landed and saw a large crowd, he had compassion on them and healed their sick.–Matthew 14:13-14 NIV

> **Grieving is not for Wimps!**

SOCIAL / RELATIONSHIPS BALANCE

Birthmothers hold a unique relationship after adoption has been chosen. A new life title as Mother and Birthmother (whether you chose to engage it or deny it), means that you have a new identity. The relationships you will have will be different than before. Some will be strengthened, some will end totally, some will start, and some will be very different. You may feel happy or hurt by these changing relationships. One thing we know about Jesus' life on earth, He was always reaching out to touch the lives of others in a positive way. You can too. Honesty, respect, forgiveness, with a commitment to being the best role model to others, should be the foundations to your new relationship dynamics.

> **How will you cope? Be true to who you are. You are God's child.**

Activity:

What are the new relationships in your life now?

How have you adjusted to the new role of Birthmother when you are in a social situation?

How are you coping?

The effort to rebalance the five areas will take a thoughtful and intentional plan. What can you do to restore each of those areas to enable you to feel balanced again?

Activity

Set at least two realistic goals for immediate action to restore balance to your life.

Intellectual

1.

2.

Emotional

1.

2.

Physical

1.

2.

Spiritual

1.

2.

Social/Relationships

1.

2.

Set at least two long-term and measurable goals to restore balance to your life.

Intellectual

1.

2.

Emotional

1.

2.

Physical

1.

2.

Spiritual

1.

2.

Social/Relationships

1.

2.

WHAT ELSE CAN I DO TO FEEL BETTER?

Be a good steward of the resources that are provided by others. Take time off and allow your body to readjust to the new reality that is being a Birthmother. The balance of these five elements: Intellectual, Emotional, Physical, Spiritual, and Social through Relationships which were discussed in a previous segment, are distorted during profound grief.

Set up a routine of eating regularly. Ensure you are eating nutritionally balanced meals. Sleep at least six to eight hours every night. Stay active without getting exhausted from the effort. Weekends are not an excuse to change the routine dramatically. The more opportunity you have to stabilize your health, the better you will feel.

CHAPTER 4

PLANS

Plans Are a Key Element to Moving Forward.

> **Life plans are not always our plans, but they are God's plan. Embrace your journey with joy.**

*O*ne of the scriptures that has driven this project is: *For I know the plans I have for you, declares the Lord. Plans to prosper you and not to harm you, plans to give you hope and a future. Then you will call on me and come and pray to me, and I will listen to you. You will seek me and find me when you seek me with all your heart.–* Jeremiah 29: 11-14 NIV

We hope that you have seen the care plan that Heather Finney designed and published for Birthmothers. A copy is available at www.BravePenny.com. Look for things to add to or mark off the plan that will help you see the progress you have made.

PLANS

Each letter of **PLANS** is an action item that can assist you in walking through the rest of your life.

P: Pray.

Acknowledge God as your Heavenly Father. He loves you more than our human minds can comprehend. He will not abandon you. He will not fail you. He will lead you. He will affirm you if you seek His will in your life.

Activity:

Set aside a time to pray each day at the same time.

Begin by saying (out loud or silently) that God is Sovereign, Holy, and a loving God. (Honor Him as your God.)

Thank Him for the blessings in your life. For health, medical care, shelter, food, friends, freedoms, and all the things that surround you and make you feel safe.

Ask for your heart's desire. What you may desire may not be God's will for your life. If you trust him, He will guide you. He is all wise, and His timing and direction for you may not be the same as you wish for them to be. Be patient and wait upon the Lord.

Listen, through reading Scripture for His wisdom to fill your life. Spend a few minutes just being quiet and being in God's presence.

Finally, end the prayer by committing yourself to His will. Be willing to be open to His changing your heart. Tell Him you trust Him. Then do that.

Activity

List 3 things that are your heart's desire.

1.

2.

3.

Keep a prayer journal.

Perhaps download a daily bible study program that includes prayer and praise.

L: Listen like Lazarus

Lazarus was a friend of Jesus. He died and was called back to life by Jesus. Looking at the story of Lazarus's death teaches some very important lessons. As was the custom of the time, Lazarus's body was wrapped and placed in a tomb very soon after death. Three days later, Jesus came to the town where his friend lived. The family of Lazarus was unhappy that Jesus had not come sooner to save Lazarus from death. Jesus assured them that He would be glorified, even in the death of His friend.

Jesus went to the tomb. He asked that the rock at the door of the tomb be removed. He called Lazarus by name.

"Lazarus, come out." Imagine for a moment that the sadness and grief that you may be feeling or have experienced is like the burial wrappings that Lazarus was wrapped in as he laid in the tomb for three days. Bindings of sadness, guilt, shame, and emptiness are holding you and hindering you from reentering a joy-filled life.

Lazarus heard Jesus calling, and he responded. Jesus called to him. He made the effort to come to the door of the burial tomb. Lazarus must have slowly sat up, he carefully stood, and then inched his way toward the door of the tomb. He pressed on, inch by inch, until he reached the tomb opening. When he appeared at the door of the tomb, there was an immediate response from others. They came to help him, to free him of the bindings. His effort had gotten him to the place of re-entry into life. A Birthmother's bindings come in the form of emotional and physical wrappings that need to be gently unwound so that she can re-enter life. Hear God's call, sit up, stand up, and then take tiny steps. Others will welcome you into the new chapter of your life when you are brave enough to move toward the entrance to your new life.

Activity:

Locate a Bible and read the story of Lazarus. (Or look it up on the web.)

In the New Testament, John 11:1-45.

Activity:

List your tiny steps to the door of your new life.

1.

2.

3.

A: Take Action.

Using your plan, explore wise actions that will empower you. These may include healthy ways to share in the love of your child and with the adoptive parents. Find common ground. Affirm that God is being glorified through this life-changing circumstance.

Old coping skills that are not really helpful can be easy to fall into. This is the time for a fresh look at how to cope in healthy ways.

Activity:

Review your plans for the day, week, and month. Set realistic goals for yourself that will move you forward into the new chapter of your life.

Day:

Week:

Month:

N: No Negative Thoughts.

It is easy to fall into the trap of questioning, condemning, and allowing destructive thought patterns to become the constant background noise of life. Do not give "prime time" to negative thoughts. Do not try to silence the negative thoughts with alcohol or drugs or withdrawal from life. Shout them down with praises to God. Affirmations of your decisions should be on your lips every day. Sing a praise song!

Activity:

List 10 things that make you happy.

1.   6.

2.   7.

3.   8.

4.   9.

5.   10.

Choose at least one of these every day. Focus on joy in a healthy way.

> **Even if it is just for a moment, let yourself experience the joy of joy.**

S: Simplify

There was a saying, "Keep It Simple, Sister." The KISS method of living makes room for the essentials of life. Take care of yourself by eating balanced meals, hydrating

> **Value God, Yourself, and Others.**

with water, getting six to eight hours of sleep, and setting a routine and sticking with it as much as possible. Recognize that the best and most lasting things in life are the relationships you build and maintain.

Activity:

List 2 goals for taking care of yourself.

1.

2.

Make a Plan! Review the Plan! Share your plan with another Birthmother.

Journal the details of your plan.

Create your own calendar to record events, goals and achievements. Visible progress inspires.

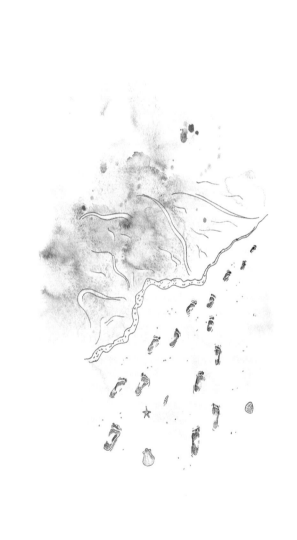

GOD'S PLAN

I hold tightly to your hands
Praying one day you will understand
Why this was always a part of God's plan.
I know this plan is not one the world will always
understand.
Just remember Our God understands.
This is not the way we meant to meet.
However here you're beside me
All grown up
And Brave as can be.
If you ever wonder why I chose adoption for us both,
Just look to His Word
And there you will see
He has a plan for you
Just like He has a plan for me.
I know it's not easy to always see.
However, here we are
Now in this scene
God's plan was for us to meet.

Heather Finney

SERENITY PRAYER

God,

Grant me the serenity to accept

The things I cannot change,

The courage to change the things I can;

And the wisdom to know the difference.

Living one day at a time;

Enjoying one moment at a time;

Accepting hardship as a pathway to peace;

Taking as Jesus did

This sinful world as it is,

Not as I would have it

Trusting that You will make all things right

If I surrender to Your will;

So that I may be reasonably happy in this life

And supremely happy with you

Forever in the next.

Amen

Reinhold Neibur

CHAPTER 5

BIBLICAL MODELS FOR PREGNANCY

MARY, THE MOTHER OF JESUS

This is a two-fold explanation about Mary. The first part of the story is God's role. God created an Open Adoption when he gifted His son Jesus to Mary and Joseph. Mary did bear her child, but Jesus was God's son first and always. He sent His son to earth via Mary. God knows what it feels like to gift a child to another family to nurture and raise.

The second part of the story is Mary's role. Her "unplanned" pregnancy was God's planned pregnancy. Although Mary and Joseph were, in modern language, engaged, they had not planned on a pregnancy at that point in their relationship. However, as in the story of Lazarus, even in the midst of unexpected human events, God can be and was glorified. Mary was the vessel of a mighty story. She was obedient to carry her child. She trusted God. She sought wisdom from others. She took on the dual role of Birthmother and Adoptive Mother to Jesus.

Conception is a miracle above all else. The biology and chemistry of conception have been well documented in medical books for decades, but the miracle of that design is God's handiwork. Only He could have designed such a perfect union of cells to create life. The Birthmother becomes the leading lady in the drama that happens for the next nine months. She supplies the nourishment and life support to two tiny cells that develop into a living, breathing baby, a true miracle and one that God had a hand in from the start. The honor to care and provide the gestation support to an infant is a testimony of God's trust in the Birthmother. He knew and wanted her to be the vessel for this important work. It may not have felt like a planned pregnancy to you, but it was to God. When the miracle of conception occurred, He knew you were the one and only woman for this job.

Mary's model for us unfolds as she wisely sought the counsel and support of other women. The wisest thing a Birthmother can do is to seek resources, knowledge, and wisdom from others who can provide help through this life-changing chapter of her life.

Read Luke 1:30-41, which describes Mary's visit with her pregnant cousin Elizabeth.

AMAZING GRACE

It is our prayer in writing this Grief Recovery Guide for Birthmothers that each will see God's provision and care for them as they walk through this process.

God smiled the day you were conceived. He smiled the day you were born. He smiled when you made the brave decision to carry your child. He and the angels above sang with joy when a child—your child—was born. You may not have seen His smile or heard the angels, but that did occur. Joy abounds in new life. Allow yourself the gift of believing the truth that God loves you. God has blessed you with the miracle of life.

How do we know that? Biblically that is what happened when Mary gave birth. Angels (The Heavenly Host) sang when the announcement of the birth of Jesus was made to the shepherds. Read Luke 2:1-14.

But before all of that, the message to the Birthmother, Mary, was, "Fear Not!" *(see Luke 1:30). Don't be afraid. Reflect on your pregnancy and let yourself feel joy because of your choice to share your child through adoption. See it as alignment with God's plan for you.

Chapter 6

Taking Care of Yourself

*T*he formula for contentment and balance.

W 2 + T 2 = Balance

W 2 + T 2. Weep, Write, Think, Talk. Do all four in equal portions to rebalance life and to facilitate the path to living contently in the next chapter of your life. Often one of the parts of the equation is avoided and discounted. Researchers find that balance and contentment are more quickly achieved if all four of the elements are addressed.

Weep

If you feel like you can't stop crying if you start, then set the timer and cry. You <u>must</u>, however, hydrate if you cry for more than 15 minutes. If you cry for an hour, and you fail to hydrate, you can become seriously dehydrated. When that occurs, your brain does not work properly. You will not be able to think clearly. YOU MUST HYDRATE! DRINK WATER!

The tears shed from grief have different chemicals than those resulting from an injury. Crying rids your body of toxins. It is good for you to cry. Jesus wept, and so should you. John Chapter 11 explains that when Jesus arrived, He was told by the sisters, Mary and Martha that Lazarus had died. Hearing the news was a profound loss for Jesus.

Jesus wept.–John 11:35. KJB

WRITE

Write

Journaling is the common form of writing to express your grief. Writing letters to yourself, others, or about the loss, is another form of expression that works as well as journaling. Most people find that writing vents emotional pressure. The journal entries are for no one to read but you. You may never need to read them again after writing them or you may re-read them often as a method of calming yourself in the midst of an emotional storm. When you write, the words do not have to be in complete sentences or be spelled correctly or in paragraph form. Sometimes the words just need to be written. Write! Write about how you feel, write about your disappointment, your joys, your expectations, and your hopes. Allow any thought that "feels like it is constantly playing over and over in your mind" to be written. Capture the memories of the hours and the days of birth and transitioning to the adoptive parents if those things seem to be constantly on your mind. Write the description in detail as often as you need to so that you will have recorded the events. This process allows the paper to be the holding place and not the constant recycling in your mind that causes you distress. If you have trouble sleeping, journal what is on your mind and what is keeping you awake at night. Write until the distraction or heavy emotion has been fully relieved from your mind.

We recommend writing by hand as the most helpful form because it allows for the size and spacing of words and letters to express the emotions too. However, if you work better with a computer as your best media to express your feelings, type.

If you are an artist, the expression of your inner thoughts may best be presented in drawings or in art form. Express your feelings through your hands if that kind of activity helps you to express your emotions.

Activity:

See the list of words in Chapter 3. Select the words that describe the feelings you find blocking your pathway to contentment.

1. Write 6 words that describe how you feel today.

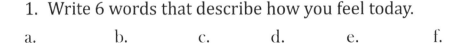
a.   b.   c.   d.   e.   f.

2. Write at least one sentence that explains each word.

a.

b.

c.

d.

e.

f.

REPEAT THIS ACTIVITY SEVERAL TIMES OVER THE NEXT FEW WEEKS AND MONTHS. YOU MAY FIND OVER TIME THAT WORDS OF JOY BEGIN TO BE LISTED MORE FREQUENTLY THAN SAD ONES.

THINK

Think

If you thought the first two parts of the formula were tough (Weep and Write) the think portions may actually be easy now. Writing about your emotion has required you to think about them. The next step is thinking how you will recall your life-changing decision. How will the life-changing decision affect the rest of your life?

Thoughts to live by

There is a concept called "inner decisions." Often unspoken or even without conscious realization of the decision, the individual *decides* something and lives it out. For example, you may know someone who is always on time, if not five minutes early. Never late! The person lives by the inner decision to always be on time. Some inner decisions are healthy and positive and others are not beneficial to our wellbeing. Inner decisions may influence relationships, trust, risk taking, eating habits, commitments to follow through on promises, and much more.

Activity: A

What are your inner decisions? How do they affect your life? Are there some new inner decisions that would lead you to a happier life?

List at least 3 inner decisions that you live by now.

1.

2.

3.

Are there some new inner decisions that you should be making now?

Your goal in this activity is to be honest in your thinking.

Activity: B

Spend some time thinking about how your choice of adoption will affect your life.

Will you be more compassionate?

Will you allow this event to make you constantly sad?

Will you choose to be content and joyful?

Will you value relationships more?

Will you decide to set healthy goals for things to achieve?

What will you think about?

TALK

Talk

The fourth portion of the formula is talk. Talk about your journey with someone you can trust (family, friend, clergy, counselor, social worker, or an adoption counselor). Let the words act as the pressure release that will bring you peace and contentment. Don't allow yourself to yield to negative thoughts by ignoring this important step.

<u>Talk it out with God.</u> He will respond to you. When you spend time with God, He can fully reveal His plan for your life. This shifts your focus from you to God. When we focus on God, He leads, affirms, and pours joy into our souls.

Talk about your hopes, your future, and your goals. Believe in them, seek them; talk about your plan. If you are in an open adoption, talk about your plans for your future and for the future relationship with your child. If your adoption is closed, talk about how you are living one day at a time and being thankful for the opportunity to have been a Birthmother who blessed another family.

Activity:

Find a support group or trusted friend(s) with whom you can talk. Share your heart.

SETTING GOOD BOUNDARIES

Setting good boundaries is one of those skills that we work on throughout life. Taking the time to think through decisions that will protect you, enhance you, shield you, and yet allow you to be fully yourself will always be a part of the challenge of living. As a Birthmother, your responsibility for wise decisions is magnified. To live responsibly will affect not only you but also the other participants in the adoption. Be a model to others. Live contently, taking care of yourself and others, and let God do His healing work in your life.

Seeking other creative solutions to living wisely is not easy. Sometimes just saying "NO" feels like the hardest word to say.

ARE YOU TIRED?

We hear the shouts from all who read this. "**YES!!**"

"I just had a baby. I am in transition from Mother to Birthmother. My body was wired physically and emotionally to nurture a child. I have empty arms. I have a sad heart. I am struggling to find the joy. Gifting my child to another family is the hardest thing I have ever done so far in my life.

I have a whole lot of feelings that I never expected to feel. All of that is SOOO intense. Of course I am tired!!!! "

Sound like you? Your soul has been wounded by these events. It takes time for healing to occur.

WOUNDED SOUL

All of the statements about being tired are true without question, but to help you to a deeper understanding of that tiredness, read on about the Wounded Soul concept.

In the process of delivery, the female body has worked very hard. Bones shifted in the pelvis, muscles were stretched, and organs were sent into contractions that aided in the birth. They play into the body's natural need to heal and be restored post-delivery. The energy of the body is sent to those parts of the body that need healing. The blood flow and complicated chemical transformations work together to create a physical recovery. The human mind does not think, "Oh, I will concentrate on sending blood and the healing chemistry to mend the areas affected during delivery." It just happens.

I believe that God is the healer of our wounded souls. As a Christian grief facilitator, I believe that our souls sustain wounds and require healing just like our body parts. This happens without our willing it or even sending the energy to the emotionally damaged areas. When you make a painful decision or experience a loss that creates grief, think of that as a wound on the soul. A "gash," if you will, on the soul has to heal slowly and has to heal from the inside out. There will be scar tissue left as the wounds heal. The normal "energy" that you have is depleted because it is silently being

> **God trusted you with this child, this new life. What an amazing honor to be a witness to God's divine grace brought to completion through you! Honor the sacred task by taking care of yourself.**

used to bring healing to your soul. It is doubly hard for the Birthmother. First, her body has to recover from delivery and next her soul has to heal from the wound of gifting her child.

Birthmothers report that there seems to be no interest in pursuing things that would deplete their limited energy pool. They have no sense of "get up and go" or the drive to do anything but just the basics of life. They only do what has to be done because there is nothing left over. They are tired. It turns out it is explainable and natural. Give yourself time to replenish your energy pool.

Activity:

Draw your wounded soul. (Hint: there may be old wounds on your soul from previous losses that you have experienced.) Some of the wounds may be tiny entry holes but go deeply into your soul. Others may be long cuts with uneven edges.

Label each wound.

Write a description of both old and new wounds.

CHAPTER 7

I HAD A DREAM

There are many types of losses. First, let's talk about concrete losses. Concrete losses are visible to others, like death of a parent or friend. There are public acknowledgments of concrete losses that make them real to others. Then there are abstract losses, which are generally not the visible type. Abstract losses include loss of confidence, loss of security, loss of love in a broken relationship, and loss of a dream. The loss of a dream means the hopes and expectations of life cannot be experienced in the same way as anticipated.

What is a dream in this context? In the fairy tale, Prince Charming sweeps the Princess off her feet, marries her, they have children, and live happily ever after.

As an adult or as teen mother, the dream of all of that has fallen apart. When things get out of sequence or there are elements that simply do not exist, the happily ever after seems very far away. When our expectations for the ideal life do not occur, we lose our dream. We grieve that loss.

Lost dreams may take several forms. The disappointment which occurs if the adoptive family moves away resulting in infrequent visits is one type. Or the lost dream when a court ruling or other circumstances prohibit contact of any kind resulting in feelings of isolation. Lost dreams are as real as losses of a more tangible or public types of loss. It takes time and it is another part of the journey of grief recovery.

LOSSES & CHANGE
By Dr Norman Meanes

So much of life is like planning a fabulous vacation trip to Italy. You buy a bunch of guidebooks and make your wonderful plans. The Coliseum, Michelangelo's David, the Gondolas in Venice. You may learn some handy phrases in Italian too! It's all very exciting! After months of eager anticipation, the day finally arrives. You pack your bags and off you go. Several hours later the plane lands. The flight attendant announces, "Welcome to Holland!" "HOLLAND?" you exclaim. "What do you mean, Holland? I signed up for Italy! I'm supposed to be in Italy! All my life I dreamed of going to Italy!"

But ... there has been a change in the flight plan. The plane landed in Holland and there you must stay.

The important thing is, they didn't take you to a horrible, disgusting, filthy place, full of pestilence, famine, and disease. It's just a DIFFERENT place. So now you must go out and buy new guidebooks. You must learn a new language, and you will meet a whole new group of people you never would have met in Italy. It's just a different place. It's slower paced than Italy, less flashy than Italy. But after you have been there for a while and you catch your breath, you look around and you begin to noitice that Holland has windmills, and Holland has tulips. And Holland even has Rembrandts.

But everyone you meet is busy, going and coming from Italy and bragging about what a wonderful time they had there. And for the rest of your life, you will say, "Yes that's where I was susposed to go. That's what I had planned." The pain of that will never, ever go away, because the loss of that dream is a very significant loss. But if you spend the rest of your life mourning the fact that you didn't get to Italy, you'll never be free to enjoy the very special and lovely things about Holland.

God promises to live in the "Hollands" of our life, as well as the Italys—if we allow Him in. God knows where we are and loves us anyway. So let the blessings and treasures of Holland come into your life through your relationship with Jesus.

Redemptions

When Christ died for us, He created a redemptive element in our eternal life that did not exist before. He redeemed each of us who choose to be His adopted brothers and sisters in faith so that we could enjoy eternity with our Heavenly Father. Our all-powerful God can redeem, renew, release, and forgive us of the sins, when we ask Him to come into our lives. Everyone who commits their life to God is God's adopted child. We are welcome to the table as equal heirs of eternal life.

CHAPTER 8

HOW DO I EXPLAIN WHAT HAPPENED?

There will be people who will ask about your pregnancy. They will expect to see you radiant as a new mother, showing off your child or at least having current pictures. They will ask how you are doing as a new mother. They may confront you with heavy judgment about the decision you have made. How do you respond to those questions and occasional attacks?

Take a deep breath and respond in love. It is Hard to do! You will be blessed if you do it!

You may want to write out the response. Each decision is based on many elements. They are personal and deep. You do not HAVE to explain. Some mothers have shared with us their responses.

I used the phrase: "I gifted my child into adoption." I made one of the most difficult decisions of my life. I know it was the best one for my child and for me. My child has joined another family as their child. I am trusting God for my future and for the future of my child.

It was the right thing to do. I can't tell you in detail how I came to the decision. Please understand that although it was a difficult decision to choose adoption, I know it was the right one.

Life is difficult in so many ways. The journey that brought me to giving birth to my child was one that I did not choose or perhaps would not have chosen. However, I carefully considered the future and chose this option of adoption as the best one. Please trust me that I have done the best thing for me.

I understand my decision might not have been your decision under the same circumstances. But I know that God will be glorified in my obedience to make this choice.

Activity:

Script <u>your</u> reply.

How do I explain how I made my decision?

The complexity of making a decision to choose adoption is often described as "indescribable." No simple set of words, phrases, or sentences can actually say what and how you came to the decision. If you struggle with this, you are not alone. It is interesting how the most important decision of our life is one that is nearly impossible to put into words. Be OK with that.

WHAT DO I DO NOW?

Your first new job as a Birthmother.

How can the Birthmother aid in bonding with an adoptive Mother in an open adoption?

Because it is necessary for the child to find equal comfort in the arms that enfold it, whether Birthmother or adoptive family member, careful planning for the gentle transition is necessary. The baby has heard a heartbeat

> **You can now use the tools that we have presented in this booklet to press into the future.**

associated sounds and movements during the gestation that have become assuring and familiar. After birth, the world assaults the child with new sensations such as temperature changes, the feel of clothing, oral intake of food, sound, and smells. The heartbeat of the mother is one of those things that has been a reassuring pattern and with a calming effect for the child. A new heartbeat, smell, and motion add to the baby's adjustment factors. In order to reduce the stress on the baby, the early hours and days after delivery should be shared between the two mothers if possible so that the changes are not too abrupt. Have a discussion about post-birth activities with your health care professional if you have not delivered your child

> **God did not say life would be easy. He did promise to be with us.**

.....And Lo! I am with you always, even unto the ends of the earth. Amen. - Matthew 28:20 KJB

Trust and ask God for guidance every day. Plan, take good care of yourself, and open yourself to new opportunities and experiences. You have learned a lot and you are in a unique position to pass on your knowledge and wisdom to others. Be God's messenger of hope to others.

> **Smile, God Loves You!**
>
> **Grief is normal after a life-changing event. It is what the Birthmother does with her grief that makes her brave. Don't bury it, deny it, or ignore it. Place it in God's hands.**

Psalm 23 was written to be a passage of comfort. As you SLOWLY read each line, visualize the picture presented in the Psalm and sense the contentment that is being presented.

English Standard Version

The Lord Is My Shepherd

A Psalm of David.

1 The Lord is my shepherd; I shall not want.
2 He makes me lie down in green pastures.
He leads me beside still waters.[a]
3 He restores my soul.
He leads me in paths of righteousness[b]
for his name's sake.

4 Even though I walk through the valley of the shadow of death,[c]
I will fear no evil,
for you are with me;
your rod and your staff,
they comfort me.

5You prepare a table before me
in the presence of my enemies;
you anoint my head with oil;
my cup overflows.
6Surely[d] goodness and mercy[e] shall follow me
all the days of my life,
and I shall dwell[f] in the house of the Lord
forever.[g]

God leads us to green pastures and quiet waters. He knows that we walk deep valleys that have shadows of darkness over them, but ahead, there is a grand table set just for each of us. It is a table with bowls of blessings, platters of grace, and cups of sweet redemptive love. Push on to the table. HE is holding a place at the table for you.

We are Survivors!!!

The difficult part on the road to recovery is deciding....
How do I fit what has happened in my life into the rest of my life?

CHAPTER 9

IS THERE CLOSURE?

The answer is "No." But there is Contentment.

The word "closure" came into use several decades ago. People were looking for a term to describe an "end" of things that were painful or difficult. Closure when used in an adoption would have to be converted to contentment. Contentment would be an end of the emotional spikes and valleys. It would be peace through acceptance of circumstances as they are: not wishing for a different yesterday, but resting in the reality of today.

There will be no closure in an open, semi-closed, or closed adoption as long as at least one of the Birthmother, child, adoptive parent/s, and families is still living. Don't look for closure or hope to find it. Look for Contentment. God wired our heart to yearn for His plan to be fully and wholly completed. When we are in His plan, we yearn to glorify God by our actions and our choices. It is in His plan that we can find contentment. Contentment is knowing that you have been obedient and you have been loving to others. Choose to be content.

THE GOODBYE THAT NEVER ENDS

Every time I see your face

I am touched by God's amazing grace.

I miss you deeply when I walk away

Saying goodbye brings me back to a dark place.

The love I have for you is deep

So each time we meet

The dark place fills with the light of your face.

I know that it is hard, my sweet child,

Not seeing you at all would be much worse.

So when I cry it's a mix

Tears of pain washed away by tears of joy

I know our moments together are fleeting.

As each one passes

And the goodbyes are said,

The foundation is strengthened

Because each time love wins again,

So to the Father I am thankful

For the goodbye that never ends.

Revision of When Grief Walks In

by Heather Finney

CONDITIONAL GOODBYES

In Open or Closed Adoptions, events take on conditional goodbyes. It is important to understand that goodbyes take on a different context than is generally expected.

Activity: Fill in the Goodbye Marker Chart. Label the markers with events you can foresee that will be "another goodbye." Labels might include: first tooth, first word, walking, and first day in school. You may also want to do the second chart on the bottom for long-term events like driver's license and high school graduation.

Goodbye Marker Chart

_/___/___/___/___/___/___/___/___/___/

_/___/___/___/___/___/___/___/___/___/

THE LIFE OF "SHOULD HAVE".

There will always be a temptation to apply the "Should Have" method of guilt and accusation to many situation in our lives. The Should Have method is typically, "I should have done X, I should have said X, they should have known X, or they should have responded in X way." A very savvy teacher once was quoted as saying, "Don't Should on me!" when talking to a person who had listed several regrets about a particular situation. The teacher went on to say. "You did what you thought at the time was the best you could do." Hindsight is 20/20. Future sight is 0/0.

> **The difficult part of the road ahead is deciding how to fit this decision into the rest of your life.**

The "shoulds" of life are easy to point to. The decision to not blame yourself and others, but to find God's solution is the real mark of maturity in faith. God will arm you with the strength you will need when "shoulds" occur. Abandon the "Should Have" view of life. Your prayer now and in the future is to lean into the loving provision that God brings to every situation. Trust God.

CHAPTER 10

ADOPTIVE PARENTS – OPEN ADOPTIONS

ASK, AND IT WILL BE GIVEN TO YOU;
SEEK, AND YOU WILL FIND; KNOCK,
AND IT WILL BE OPENED TO YOU. -
MATTHEW 7:7 ESB

*H*ow do you choose the adoptive parents in an Open Adoption?

Or perhaps the question should be: "How will God choose them?" Only He knows.

As you walk the new journey of Birthmother, either prior to the birth of your child or after your child is born, the decision of who will be the lifelong influence as adoptive parents to your birth child is daunting. Many resources are available to you through adoption agencies, churches, friends, social workers, hospital staff, or support groups. There is not one tried and true solution that all Birthmothers can rely upon for selection except one. Pray earnestly for God to reveal to you the right choice, not the one that is necessarily the easiest or most obvious, but the one that God has already selected for you and your child. Be open to input from others, but don't be trapped by their input. Pray for peace in your choice. There is a family waiting for your child. Trust God to direct you to them.

It is a good idea to think through the desires of your heart for your child. What elements do you desire for your child to experience?

Christian parents, loving home environment, stability, openness to the idea of sharing with you an open adoption relationship, ability to express to you their commitment and desire to parent your birth child, and trust are just a few of the possible items on your list. Think through your list to use as a basis for choice of adoptive parents. The list will help you to know that you have made the best choice for your birth child.

If you have experienced a closed adoption, your input on selection of adoptive parents was not an option. Trust and pray that your child has been placed with a family that has loved, appreciated, and celebrated the gift that you enabled them to receive.

Activity:

What are you/were you looking for in adoptive parents?

1.

2

3

4

5

Once you have made your selection, trust and pray that God will affirm and validate your choice over and over again for you. The decision is legally binding and irrevocable. Let go when that has occurred. Let God take it from there. Your job is to willingly share, without resentment or jealously, your birth child. Ask God for the grace to do that and to do it well. Your new role of birthmother and the expression of your love for your birth child is a model of unselfish love, unconditionally lived out. Choose wisely and let God lead you to the parents who will receive, value, and share your gift—your birth child.

HOW COULD THE ADOPTIVE MOTHER/ FAMILY REACT?

Adoptive parents come with all kinds of personalities, resources, and convictions. You may find some whose actions are fully and carefully presented in love toward you. You may also find jealously, distancing, and severing of contact a reality as well.

Adoptive mother depression has been documented. This idea that the adoptive mother or family can struggle with depression is somewhat startling but statistically true. Adoptive mothers also share the common emotion or health issue of depression. When the outsider would think, "She should be so happy. How could she possibly be depressed?" The reality, like all things in life, may originate from contemplation of her ability to do something well. To decide to adopt and then actually realize that it is life changing and challenging. That action can sometimes be accompanied by questions that turn into depression. Questions like: "Will I be able to fully parent this child? What will happen if I miss something that other parents just do naturally? How can I be sure that I can meet the expectations of others?" (See article listed in the reference section on depression of adoptive parents.) There are resources to help. If a situation should occur, see a health care professional or other resources through an adoption agency. You, as a Birthmother, should not be responsible for fixing this, but you can recognize and be aware that depression can occur in adoptive parents.

When things change

It is impossible to anticipate the changes that will occur in the adopting family or in the life of the Birthmother. The one sure thing about life is that there will be changes. Some changes may be anticipated and some, suddenly thrust, unexpectedly upon us. Our response can fall into several categories: anger, frustration, a sense of helplessness, delight, joy, acceptance, and contentment. Often, changes in our life are a complex mix of all of the above and more. How we choose to live out the circumstances is a reflection of our choice to choose God in trust and in faithfulness or to take on the battle on our own. The human fallback plan is to take it on! Look to our own strength and determination (as mentioned in the first chapter) to solve the problem or overcome the situation! This is not God's way. Trust Him, being obedient and allowing God to be the Father He is, is a difficult response, but one that creates lasting contentment.

What happens if death, accident, transfer to a new location, addition of other siblings, or divorce of the adoptive parents occur? These possibilities cannot be anticipated, nor should there be an "action plan" in place. The chances of these occurring are relatively low.

> **Your purpose was to be the vessel which allowed God's precious child to be born. You have a purpose and God will honor that purpose.**

Do not spend your energy trying to map out the decision for an unknown event. If these or some other unexpected issues occur, trust God to walk you through them. He has brought you through life so far. He will not abandon you now. Trust that all things will come under his watchful care.

We know that all things work together for good to them that love God, to them who are called according to His purpose.–Romans 8:28 KJB

SUICIDE

The topic of suicide is always difficult to talk about. Suicide rates are measurably higher in Birthmothers than in other segments of the female population. Suicide is the third highest cause of death in young adults.

<u>Suicide is not the answer.</u> Even though you can't see the future, know that God does see the future and has a plan already laid in place. All you have to do is follow His will.

<u>What does "Follow His Will" mean?</u> Show up, have a good attitude, try to do the right thing, work hard on any task, keep your word so that people around you can trust you, and trust God to reveal His plan to you when it is time to do so. Be open to His leading and to positive suggestions from others.

<u>Seek professional help.</u> Talk to someone who is trained to support you during this time. It is not in God's Plan for

you as a Birthmother to leave the child or adoptive parents with the burden of your death. As hard as this situation is, suicide is not a solution. It will not make life easier or better for others. You may have significant emotional pain, but it is not God's plan for a Birthmother to multiply that pain into the lives of others. One death creates multiple grief experiences for those who are left behind. The results of suicide are the complete opposite of God's plan for a Birthmother and her adoption. Be courageous and once again choose life. Because this time, it is your own life you choose. You as a Birthmother are divinely chosen by God. Suicide is NOT the answer.

What to do if you feel suicidal:
1. Seek professional medical help.
   a. Call 800-273-8255 Suicide Hot Line
   b. Or contact adoption support services

BIRTHMOTHER TO BIRTHMOTHER:

I EXPERIENCED DEPRESSION. I TRIED EVERYTHING TO PREVENT IT BEFOREHAND THROUGH PRAYER, READING GOD'S WORD, TALKING TO MY COUNSELOR, EXERCISING, AND EATING RIGHT. BUT NOTHING COULD STOP THE "DOWN SPIRALING" EFFECT OF DEPRESSION. I JUST WANTED TO DIE AND I COULD NOT STOP THE FEELINGS. I KNOW IT WAS A COMBINATION OF HORMONES AND GRIEF. SO I STARTED MEDICATION. I AM GLAD I DID. I EXPERIENCED RELIEF AND WAS ABLE TO PROCESS MY FEELINGS IN A HEALTHIER WAY. SO DON'T BE AFRAID TO GET HELP THROUGH MEDICATION AND COUNSELING. IT WILL HELP YOUR GRIEF.–ANNA

Sometimes we need a bridge to get us from dark places and dark times into the light. Counseling and medications can often provide that bridge to contentment that God wants for us.

Birthfathers and Birth Families Members

This workbook was specifically designed for Birthmothers. It does demand the recognition that there are Birthfathers who grieve and grieve deeply when adoption is chosen. The Birthfather may experience many of the same emotional feelings that the Birthmother experiences. The biological and physical changes from pregnancy notwithstanding, the Birthfather's role, if he chooses to participate, can be very impactful on the overall ability of the Birthmother to recover in a healthy way. We invite the Birthfathers to be a part of this journey, to utilize the workbook and to find God's guiding grace.

Birth Grandparents grieve deeply. It is wise to acknowledge the deep yearning of the grandparents who have limited or no contact with their grandchild, which creates a lifelong impact of grief. We also invite them to share in the information in this workbook. God's Model, Wounded Soul, forgiveness, and many other topics or concepts apply to the extended family.

Activity:

As a Birthfather or as a Birth Grandparent or Birth-family member, journal your feelings or write letters about your loss.

Samantha Johnson from Living Alternatives in Texas wrote the following:

God's design is for woman to be married and get pregnant and have babies. So when we make decisions or things happen outside of God's original design there is grief. It was never in God's design for a woman to have sex outside of marriage and babies were not to be conceived outside of the covenant of marriage. So there is grief associated with the redemptive decision to place a baby for adoption (actually to parent too). You know even the chemicals/

hormones in a woman's body are all designed to parent/ love/attach to a baby that is born to us. God is so amazing to make ways of redemption in our sinful acts, though. Just like the grief of death, God's original design for man was not death, so now we grieve that loss.

"A Birthmother is an invaluable part of a child's life. She is chosen by the Lord, because she has all the parts in her blood line that are needed to carry out God's plan for a child. In secret she carries this life for nine short months. A Birthmother is a person to be thankful for, to be grateful for, and hold in admiration."

Heather Finney

ALWAYS A MOTHER

There you stand in the midst of defeat,

Holding something you can never keep.

It is an unnatural experience and a painful one too

To hold something you can never keep.

The circumstances that brought you to this moment

are now flesh and blood.

They now have tiny hands, a sweet cry, with the most

beautiful big blue eyes.

The reality grips your soul, ripping your heart into a

million pieces.

As you stand there holding something you can

never keep.

The truth is hard to bear knowing the family you

always wanted is no longer there.

This choice is going to take a Bravery this world can

never understand.

It takes a love so Brave so rare, so sweet, it brings a

mother to her knees.

To Love something you can never keep.

Is the Bravest love, I think, God has ever seen.

So even though I am not like you nor you like me, we
are one Brave Family, linked together by a love so rare,
so courageous, so patient and gracious
It takes nine months to get it here.
However, above all, we are now a family forged in a
love only God himself can create.
As I hand you this life I can never keep,
I have come to see I will always be a mother and now,
you are one too.
That's what Brave love can do.

By Heather Finney

Scripture References for Grief

When in sorrow	John 14
When men fail you	Psalm 27
When you worry	Matthew 6:19-34
When you are in danger	Psalm 91
When God seems far away	Psalm 139
When your faith needs stirring	Hebrews 11
When you are alone and fearful	Psalm 23
When you grow bitter and critical	I Corrinthians 13
When you feel down and out	Romans 8:31
When you want courage for a task	Joshua 1
If you are depressed	Psalm 27
If you are losing confidence in people	I Corinthians 13
If people seem unkind	John 15

If you are discouraged about your
work   Psalm 126

If you are becoming too self cen-
tered   Psalm 19

Dealing with fear   Psalm 34:7

For Security   Psalm 121:3

For assurance   Mark 8:35

For Christian assurance   Matthew 11:25-30

How to get along with others   Romans 12

Whe you have sinned   Psalm 51

Paul's secret to happiness   Colossians 3:12-17

If you want to be truthful   John15

If your packetbook is empty   Psalm 37

REFERENCES AND RESOURCES:

www.Ichooseadoption.org

C.S. Lewis	A Grief Observed
Brenda Romanchok	Impact of birthmother
Donna Paluesi	Birth Parent loss and grief
Patricia Roles	Life issues
Deborah Saberstine &	No more guilt, no
Sharon Kaplin Rossia	more grief
Mary Black	Out of the shadows into our lives? Adoption and loss the hidden grief
Evelyn Robinson	Surviving the Fires
Elizabeth Kubler-Ross	On death and Dying.
Marilyn Dickson	Grief Recovery Seminar, Northway Presbyterian Church, Dallas, TX

Sister Teresa M McIntier, RN, MS,	Life After Loss – How to help others through the grieving process
Larry Yeagley	Conducting Greif Support Groups, 1994 Edition
Carol Brooks	B.S.N Psychiatric Nurse, Adult Ministry, Christ Church, Plano, TX

Leave the past to the mercy of God

Leave the present to the love of God

Leave the future to the providence of God

Now, go in peace and serve the Lord

CPSIA information can be obtained at www.ICGtesting.com
Printed in the USA
LVOW01s0703121014

408333LV00001B/1/P